ASK ABOUT OCEANIA

Mason Crest Publishers Inc.
370 Reed Road
Broomall, Pennsylvania 19008
(866) MCP-BOOK (toll free)

First printing

1 2 3 4 5 6 7 8 9 10

Library of Congress Cataloging-in-Publication Data on file at the Library of Congress.

ISBN 1-59084-207-3
ISBN 1-59084-198-0 (series)

Printed in Malaysia.

Adapted from original concept produced by Vineyard Freepress Pty Ltd, Sydney.
Copyright © 2002 Vineyard Freepress Pty Ltd.

Project Design and Text: Valerie Hill
Consultant: Noeline Lapwood
Cartography: Peter Barker
Pre-press: Dein Miskell
Printer: Toppan Printing
Images: Noeline Lapwood Principal photographer. All images except the following: Peter Barker, Mike Langford, Maori Arts and Crafts Institute, Tamaki Maori Village, T. Mitai-Ngati, Dein Miskell, Christchurch and Canterbury Marketing, Northland Images, New Zealand Parliamentary Service Commission, Tourism Rotorua, Tourism Holdings, Tourism Auckland, Totally Wellington, Dalmation Genealogical Society, Mark Samson, Decca Records, New Zealand Herald, AP/AAP, Vineyard Stock.

COVER: Maori cultural dancer in traditional dress.

TITLE PAGE: Detail. Maori crafts of wood carving, painting and flax weaving. The curved motif is taken from the new frond of a fern.

CONTENTS: Rock fishing.

INTRODUCTION: Schoolgirls in the library in an Auckland primary school.

New Zealand

MASON CREST PUBLISHERS

CONTENTS

MODERN NEW ZEALAND

DAILY LIFE

INTRODUCTION

NEW ZEALAND is the most southern of the Pacific islands. Its dramatic landscape varies from volcanic hot spots in the north to fjords and glaciers in the south. But there are also farms on gentle hills where livestock thrive. Always dependent on its rich produce, the country makes full use of up-to-date research and communications systems.

The practical and innovative New Zealanders, despite their small population, are known throughout the world for their courage in battle, their passion for a clean environment, and their love of invention. Two different cultures, Maori and British, have lived together for only two hundred years and continue to find ways to strengthen their nation. In this beautiful land children can enjoy both freedom and education.

▲ Weta

NEW ZEALAND

The islands of New Zealand lie in the south Pacific Ocean so close to the International Date Line that the eastern tip, East Cape, is the first land in the world touched by the rising sun. Isolated from the rest of the world by sea, New Zealand's nearest neighbor is Australia, 1,120 miles (1,800 kilometers) northwest across the Tasman Sea; and to the east across the vast Pacific Ocean it is 4,970 miles (8,000 kilometers) to Argentina. In the south the ice cap of Antarctica is separated from New Zealand only by the cold Southern Ocean.

The two major islands are quite different. Rain forests, bushland, and gorse share the temperate North Island with cultivated crops, which grow to the edges of cliffs and waterways. Around the coast, people enjoy beaches, bays, and islands. Hot thermal springs, mud pools, and geysers are active in the volcanic region between the now extinct volcano, Mount Taupo, and the Bay of Plenty.

The South Island is long and narrow with a granite backbone formed by the Southern Alps, which end in deep fjordlands and forests. The Alps are capped with snow all year, and in winter, gales from the Antarctic create deep snowfields and glaciers. The precipitous west coast has one of the highest rainfalls in the world. East of the Alps it is much drier. The broad pasturelands of the Canterbury Plains are formed by shale, weathering from the Alps.

▲
Giant Kauri trees, once found across the North Island, can grow to 75 feet (23 meters) around the trunk.

▼
Queenstown nestles beside the lake with the Remarkables surrounding. Farms, ski slopes, and gold mines are in the area nearby.

▲ Pohutukawa, or New Zealand Christmas Tree, North Island.

▲ The kiwi, a national symbol unique to New Zealand, is a nocturnal and flightless bird.

CLIMATE

Temperate maritime with sharp regional contrasts: Seasons are the reverse of those in the northern hemisphere, with January warmest and July coolest.

FACT FILE

Official Name: New Zealand
Official Language: English
Population: 3,864,129
Capital: Wellington
  (Population: 430,500)
Currency: New Zealand Dollar
Land Area: 103,737 sq miles
  (268,670 sq km)
Ethnic Groups: European 79.1%;
  Maori 9.7%; Others 11.2%
Religions: Anglican 24%;
  Presbyterian 18%; Roman
  Catholic 15%; Other Protestant
  10%; Unspecified 33%
Major Physical Features:
  Highest point: Aorangi-Mt Cook
  12,314 ft (3,764 m)
Territories (not shown on map):
  Antipodes Islands,
  Auckland Islands, Bounty Islands,
  Campbell Island, Chatham
  Islands, Kermadek Islands
Dependent Areas:
  Cook Islands, Niue, Tokelau
  Territorial claim in Antarctica
  (Ross Dependency—disputed)

Cape Reinga
North Cape
Ninety Mile Beach
Great Exhibition Bay
Kerikeri
Bay of Islands
Russell
Waitangi
Whangarei
SOUTH PACIFIC OCEAN
Great Barrier Island
Hauraki Gulf
Coromandel Range
Auckland
TASMAN SEA
White Island
Katikati
Bay of Plenty
East Cape
Hamilton
Tauranga
Rotorua
North Taranaki Bight
Taupo
Gisborne
Lake Taupo
NORTH ISLAND
Mahia Peninsula
New Plymouth
Mount Egmont / Taranaki
Mount Ruapehu
Napier
Hawke Bay
South Taranaki Bight
Hastings
Wanganui
Cape Farewell
NEW ZEALAND
Palmerston North
Masterton
Tasman Bay
Cook Strait
WELLINGTON
Picton
Nelson
Cape Palliser
Blenheim
Westport
SOUTH ISLAND
Greymouth
Southern Alps
Canterbury Plains
Franz Josef Glacier
Christchurch
Fox Glacier
Banks Peninsula
Aorangi - Mount Cook
Canterbury Bight
Timaru
Milford Sound
Arrowtown
Queenstown
Oamaru
Lake Te Anau
Roxburgh
Fiordland National Park
Otago Peninsula
West Cape
Dunedin
Invercargill
Foveaux Strait
Stewart Island
Southwest Cape

N
W E
S

▼ Glaciers form in
troughs between
the sharp
upthrusted
mountains of the
South Island.

km		100	200	300
miles		100		200

▲ ▼

Lake Taupo was formed by one of the largest volcanic eruptions to occur during the last 5,000 years. In the diagram below the amount of material (in cubic kilometers) ejected from Taupo is compared with other major volcanoes across the world. (Note: One cubic kilometer equals 0.24 cubic miles).

WITH POWER OF FIRE AND WATER

The islands of New Zealand were formed by the immense power of molten rock moving in the mantle beneath the earth's crust. In the North Island, volcanic eruptions pushed up islands and mountains. Lakes filled low places, and bush and grassland grew in the soil, enriched by the lava, rock, and ash that formed it in ages past. In the center of the North Island volcanoes, geysers, hot springs, and boiling mud pools remain in evidence of the great heat below.

60-100 cubic kilometers of material

3

18

0.001

1

5

| Vesuvius AD 79 | Taupo AD 186 | Krakatau 1883 | Ngauruhoe 1975 | St Helens 1980 | Pinatubo 1991 |

Upper Mantle (Lithosphere)

Mantle (Asthenosphere)

Outer Core
Inner Core

Crust

▲ Steam, heated deep within the earth, rises from fissures in the volcanic crater of White Island in the Bay of Plenty. It has been active for more than a thousand years. Sulphur was mined from it since the 1880s.

◀ Structure of the earth.

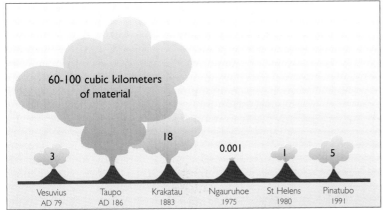

◀ No longer active, the crater of Mount Eden in Auckland is now a favorite place to play. In the center of the cone is scoria, the dull red porous stone formed by cooling lava.

Steam, rising from deep within the earth at Wairakei in the North Island is piped to a power plant. There, electric power is produced by turbines driven by geothermal energy.

The South Island was formed in a different way when great slabs of the earth's crust were forced upward and ground by solid ice glaciers to create the precipitous Southern Alps, deep fjords, and lakes. Clouds of moisture from the sea meet these mountains and release immense falls of rain that combine with melting snow to pour down waterfalls, rivers, and streams carrying shale to form the plains.

▲ Peaks of the Southern Alps rise above deep, cold, still waters of Fiordland.

▲
Granite.

▶ People shield their faces from the spray and roar of Bowen Falls as water plunges at a great pressure from a lake high in the granite peaks to Milford Sound, South Island.

▲
Turbine.

▼ A man-made hydroelectric power station creates water pressure by damming a lake or river and funneling the water through huge tubes fast enough to drive turbines and produce electric power.

▼
Sulphur.

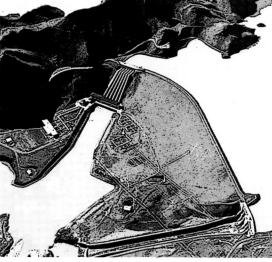

POLYNESIANS AND THE PACIFIC

New Zealand, the most southerly of the Pacific islands, has been inhabited by Maori for some six hundred years, although there are stone monuments and cave markings that suggest earlier ancient visitors. Also some Maori traditions claim they intermarried with fair-skinned *tangata whenua* (earlier people of the land). Maori are thought to be descendants of Austronesian-speaking peoples who left the Asian mainland and, living on Southeast Asian islands, gradually made their way to the Pacific Ocean islands of Polynesia (meaning "many islands"). There they settled and developed a culture of their own, adapting their beliefs and language to the new conditions and foods. In about AD 1350 some families made the incredible journey of more than 995 miles (1,600 kilometers) from Polynesia, across open sea, to the colder islands of *Aotearoa,* "Land of the Long White Cloud." They claimed territory as they landed at various points along the coast.

▲
Putatara, made of conch shell, wood, and feathers, is blown to announce important events such as the birth of a child. Conch shells, rarely found in New Zealand, probably came from tropical Polynesia.

▲ Two-hulled canoes used by Polynesians for long journeys.

MIGRATION OF MAORI ANCESTORS

The arrows on the map below show the probable route of people who, more than 4,000 years ago, began to migrate from the Asian mainland, gradually moving along a chain of Southeast Asian islands to the Polynesian islands in the Pacific Ocean and finally, about AD 1350 to New Zealand.

LEGENDS OF ANCIENT VOYAGES

- Polynesian and Maori legends tell how Maui sailed east and made the sun stay longer in the sky, discovered fire, and fished the North Island out of the sea.

- Others wonder if ancient Egyptian seafarers, Maui and Rata, inspired the Maui legends in an epic voyage from Egypt's Nile to South America and Polynesia.

- Kupe, another favorite character, is said to have made a return voyage from *Hawaiiki* (the legendary Maori homeland) to *Aotearoa.*

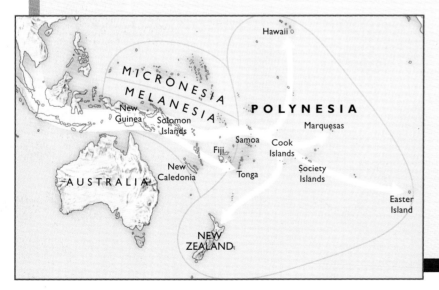

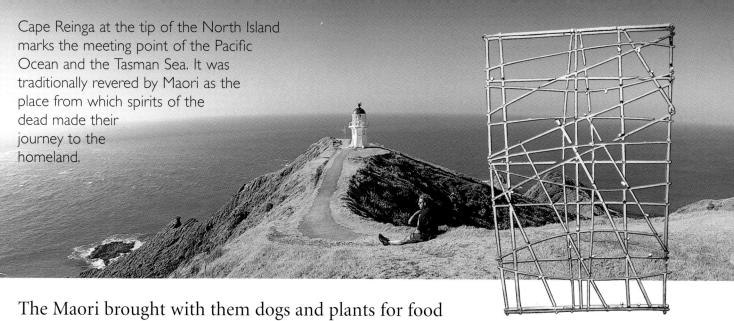

Cape Reinga at the tip of the North Island marks the meeting point of the Pacific Ocean and the Tasman Sea. It was traditionally revered by Maori as the place from which spirits of the dead made their journey to the homeland.

The Maori brought with them dogs and plants for food (taro, yams, kumera). The land was much colder than Polynesia and many crops would not grow, so they lived by fishing and hunting until the abundant birdlife became scarce. Later, most moved to the warmer north island where crops grew better. Another people, the fair-skinned Moriori, were the first inhabitants of the tiny, rugged Chatham Islands. They lived by a code of peace until enslaved by a group of Maori.

▲ Early sailing chart made in the Marshall Islands from ribs of palm leaves with different sized shells attached to mark islands. Very accurate, it was still in use in 1850.

▼ Moas, giant flightless birds, roamed the forests of New Zealand until hunted to extinction. The Maori moa-hunters often burned great swathes of forest as they stalked them. The kiwi is a species of moa.

◄ The flax plant was pounded into a soft silky fabric for clothes, woven flat for wall panels and baskets, and made into rope.

▲ Cloaks covered with flax and cabbage tree leaves gave warmth and protection from the frequent rain.

◄ Greenstone, a treasure said to have been found by Kupe.

▲ Diorama of early Maori preserving birds by smoking them.

MAORITANGA

Maoritanga means the classic Maori way of life, language, beliefs, legends, and art, which varied between tribes (or *iwi*). Within each *iwi* were close-knit families (*whanau*) that included cousins and other relatives (*hapu*). Maori were great orators and the thirty major *iwi* could recite the names of ancestors as far back as the seven great canoes (*waka*) from Polynesia. Maori lived by the laws of *tapu*. Any who broke these rules feared punishment or death by their animist gods connected with every part of life. Only rituals led by the *tohunga* (priest) could gain the approval of these gods, and he was respected and obeyed by all.

▲ Small huts (*whare*) were grouped together into villages (*kainga*). In some *kainga* there were only a few families, in others up to five hundred were grouped around a fortified hilltop (*pa*).

▶

Waka taua, war canoes, were the pride of the Maori. Cut from giant trees, they measured up to 80 feet (24 meters) long. The best wood carvers crafted the bow and stern pieces. A double row of warriors (up to 100) sped the canoes forward.

▲ Song and dance (*haka*) have strong rhythm. War dances were intended to make warriors brave and enemies afraid.

▲ Kiwi-feather cloak.

Maori *tapu* had many beliefs in common with the animist religions of Asia: customs and arts were related to belief in the power of ancestors and natural objects such as the sun, mountains, rocks, and trees. Main art forms were carving, weaving, singing, and dancing. *Utu* (revenge) for any insult caused deadly intertribal wars.

▲ As a defense against invading tribes, a *pa* or fort, was built, with trenches, earth ramparts, and palisades of wooden poles. The *pa* was often on a hill or promontory surrounded by sea, river, or swamps.

◀ *Aha*, a carved saw set with shark's teeth said to have been used to cut the flesh of defeated foes.

MOKO—HISTORY ON A FACE

A Maori carver describes the lines or shapes of the *moko*, or fully tattooed face, as the joining of godly and earthly lines. Each mark reveals the man's ancestors, family, or achievements. Tattoos were cut deep into the skin with sharp pointed bones or shells, then soot was rubbed in to color the wound black.

MOTHER'S SIDE:

RANKING
given dominion over his tribal area to north, south, east, and west of his region

FATHER'S SIDE:

Rays show position in life

Storyteller, authority on family history

Foreseeing future

At one time a warrior on both sides

Mouth rays show position from birth

Right to pass moko on to eldest son

Eldest son

Children from first marriage

Children from second marriage

Promoted from warrior to master of weaponry.

Promoted to master carver

Chief under the age of 25 years

Protected knowledge

Corresponds with nose design

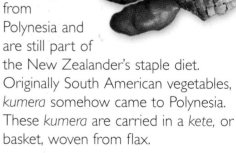

▶ *Kumera*, or sweet potatoes, were brought from Polynesia and are still part of the New Zealander's staple diet. Originally South American vegetables, *kumera* somehow came to Polynesia. These *kumera* are carried in a *kete*, or basket, woven from flax.

EUROPEANS AND THE PACIFIC

▲
Captain James Cook
(1728–1779),
brilliant English
navigator and
explorer, who landed
on the east coast of
the North Island on
6 October 1769.

By the seventeenth century, the Portuguese, Dutch, and English were traveling from Europe to Asia by sea and Columbus had reached the Americas. But New Zealand, Australia, and some smaller islands of the southern Pacific Ocean remained outside the trade routes. In 1642, sailing from the Dutch trading post in Java, the explorer Abel Janszoon Tasman reached the west coast of New Zealand's south island. He called it *Staten Landt*, but later it became known as *Novo Zeelandia* (New Zealand) after a province of Holland. Tasman's reports did not seem favorable to traders and the lands of the southern hemisphere remained a mystery to Europeans until Captain James Cook's voyages in the late 1700s.

▲ Abel Tasman, a great Dutch seaman of the seventeenth century, made this drawing in his journal. It shows Dutch ships at anchor in Tasman Bay surrounded by Maori war canoes (four sailors were killed). The Dutch were, at that time, Europe's leader in maritime trade and mapmaking.

▶ The *Endeavour*, James Cook's sturdy ship, once a humble collier (coal-carrier), proved ideal for both long voyages and coastal exploration.

▲ Cook wrote in the ship's log about his first encounter with Maori and his regret that their attack had led to some fighting. Sailing along the coast he met more friendly tribes. They exchanged food for cloth, axes, and nails (which were new to the Maori who had no metal objects).

At the time of James Cook's first Pacific voyage in the eighteenth century, Britain was the greatest maritime nation and sailed the seas, trading and setting up outposts. This was an age when Europeans had a passion for natural science. Cook's ship carried astronomers to Tahiti to observe the transit of Venus across the sun. Their quest was to calculate the earth's distance from the sun. Cook's second task, set by the British Admiralty, was to search for *Terra Australis Incognita,* "the unknown South Land," which ancient records said existed in the southern hemisphere. Before reaching Australia, Cook arrived at New Zealand on 6 October 1769.

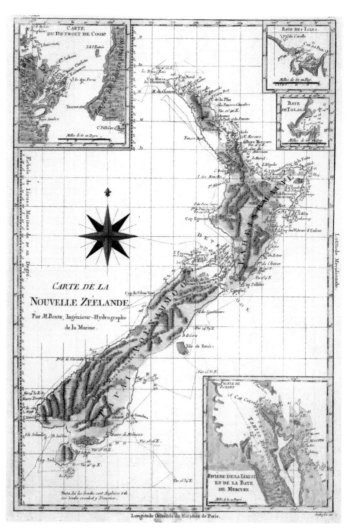

▶ This map drawn from James Cook's charts of New Zealand, showed it to be several islands, not the large southern continent.

▲ With Cook was Joseph Banks, who collected and catalogued New Zealand's unique plants and wildlife. This drawing of *kowhai* is in Banks's book, *Floralegium.*

THE COMING OF BRITISH CULTURE

James Cook's historic journey brought the first extended contact between Maori and European cultures, which had until that time followed separate paths. New Zealand knew only Polynesian culture; Britain, about the same size but across the world, was close to Europe and had undergone tumultuous changes for centuries. Britain's earliest tribes were transformed by the nations that had conquered them—Romans, Danes, and French, in turn, had ruled for nearly one thousand years. All left ideas that influenced Britain's roads, buildings, science, language, government, and law. Out of this long struggle, the British nation emerged, and by Cook's time, its culture was taking root in countries across about one quarter of the world, including New Zealand.

▶ With the English system of writing, Maori could keep written records, write letters, and read the literature of many peoples. In this letter a Maori chief set out tribal grievances and a challenge to battle!

LAND AND TREATY

When the differing Maori and European cultures came together, there was misunderstanding and conflict. European contact began badly with traders whose only interest was to profit from the natural resources, particularly sealskins and whale oil, timber and flax (for ropemaking). Cook had praised the fertile land, but it was sixty years before families, many of whom had lost farms during the Industrial Revolution, migrated to make their homes in New Zealand. With them were Christian missionaries who, though small in numbers, were leaders in setting up schools and hospitals, and had a good record for standing against injustices to Maori and settlers.

▲ Hongi Hika (center) chief of the Ngapuhi, painted during his visit to England in 1820, when he helped scholars compile the first Maori dictionary. He was presented to King George IV and received many gifts, which he exchanged in Sydney for 300 muskets. Back in New Zealand, he used them to attack his old tribal enemies. Other tribes then acquired muskets and for ten years the Maori fought one another until 60,000 had been killed.

◄ From 1790 on, sealing and whaling parties, marooned for months or years in harsh conditions, ruined Maori villages near their camps and spread diseases. Because the Maori had no natural immunity, many died.

▶ Missionaries came to the uncomfortable frontiers because they wanted to tell the "good news"—that Jesus Christ, the Son of God, loved all people. And they spoke against exploitation, whether by corrupt Europeans or in Maori practices of slavery and cannibalism. Many Maori preferred *tapu* and warrior revenge, but a few, like Te Whiti o Rongomai, took up a new life of peace that even the English found challenging (see page 21).

▶ Governor George Grey upheld the treaty during his time of office (1845–1853) and established schools and hospitals. He gained respect from Maori, but some settlers resented him. The next governor, however, did not understand the Maori and caused deep anger and hardship by his decisions.

◄ Maori farms produced wheat, oats, barley, maize, vegetables, and pigs for sale to the European population.

Land was important to both Maori and European. Both wanted secure areas to grow food, make a home, and find a sense of well-being. But neither understood the other's laws of land ownership. The British concept of one person owning, buying, or selling land was unknown to the Maori, whose tribes controlled territories inherited from ancestors or taken in war. Powerful warrior tribes had amassed much land, and some British companies took up large areas of land illegally or at unfair prices and resold at high prices. In an effort to resolve these problems, the Treaty of Waitangi was made between Maori chieftains and the British Crown on 5 February 1840. Weaknesses in the treaty have caused dissension until the present time.

▲ The Treaty of Waitangi was signed by British and Maori leaders at Resident James Busby's house at Waitangi, now called Treaty House. Forty Maori chiefs signed the treaty but others opposed it. Copies taken all over the country extended treaty terms to other tribes.

THE TREATY OF WAITANGI

- THE MAORI WERE PROMISED PROTECTION, FULL RIGHTS AS BRITISH SUBJECTS AND FULL POSSESSION OF THEIR LANDS.

- THE QUEEN OF ENGLAND WAS GRANTED FULL SOVEREIGNTY OVER THE LAND (THAT IS, NEW ZEALAND BECAME A BRITISH TERRITORY).

- ONLY THE BRITISH GOVERNMENT COULD BUY LAND AND SELL IT TO SETTLERS (MEANT TO PROTECT THE MAORI FROM EXPLOITATION).

The good intention of the treaty was flawed. It was written in English and translated into Maori but had not been clearly drafted or translated, and Maori did not understand the meaning of some key words.

▼ The City of Wellington forty-five years after it was begun by 1,000 settlers, who landed on the beach to find nothing but swamp and thick bush. Wellington was one of the "planned communities" set up on land bought by the New Zealand Company and resold to more than 18,000 British migrants.

DIVIDING THE LAND

Following the signing of the Treaty of Waitangi, shiploads of new settlers arrived from England, Scotland, and Ireland. They came to seek land, set up farms, and build towns. Gold was discovered, kauri timber and gum were major exports, and the sheep and wool industry began. Maori and migrants from other nations also worked in these new industries. The Maori grew crops for market while keeping their tribal lifestyle but increasingly resented their loss of lands. The treaty was unclear and often ignored, so that the governor was unable to control disputes about land between settlers and Maori (who also disagreed between themselves). Lawlessness increased and by 1843 led to full-scale civil war between European and Maori.

▲ Established by the Free Church of Scotland in 1848, Dunedin was given the Gaelic name for Edinburgh, capital of Scotland. Pipe bands, hard work, and orderliness reflect its Scottish beginnings.

▶ Gold discovered in the 1850s made Dunedin wealthy. Great public buildings were erected and, in their Reformation tradition of learning, the Scots built New Zealand's first university.

▲ Trees were felled with a cross-cut saw pulled back and forth by two men, then hauled by bullocks to a sawmill to be cut into lighter planks.

◀ Kauri gum, or resin, used in varnish (a hard shiny coating for wood, paintings, or other surfaces).

▲ Reenactment of a group of Irish families from Ulster arriving to settle Kati Kati, Bay of Plenty. Each family selected 40 acres for each adult and 20 acres for each child, with a minimum of 300 acres.

▶ The 20,000 gum-diggers included Maori along with Croation, Dalmatian, Chinese, and Malayan immigrants. These dancers pass on their Dalmatian culture.

▲ Planned as an English city, Christchurch was established by the Anglican Church in 1850. English names, like the River Avon and Canterbury Plains, reminded settlers of home.

▶ By the late 1800s, towns were comfortable, but pioneer bush living was lonely and primitive. Women, wherever they lived, brought order and comfort to the roughest surroundings (and tried to make the men behave better). In a rough timber camp, these ladies, dressed in their carefully laundered clothes, peel potatoes to cook over an open fire in the log chimney.

While some Maori were eager to sell their land, others, seeing the great numbers of settlers arriving, feared that they would lose all their land and refused to sell. Some developers and settlers used legal loopholes or threats to get land, forcing the government to act for them. Although the Maori tried many ways to resist or adapt, they were defeated in law and war. Some lost heart but those who had fought hardest continued to seek recognition and land.

▶ Chief Hone Heke four times cut down the British flag pole at Kororareka (now Russell). His protests sparked a long period of fierce battles known as the Maori-European Wars (1843–1881). The British won and confiscated the lands of Maori who fought.

▼ Te Whiti o Rongomai took the way of passive resistance. With Maori who had been taken, he built Parihaka, a model town whose peaceful people worked together growing crops. But the government wanted the land and over many years destroyed Parihaka. Here, soldiers are arresting ploughmen. Te Whiti and many of his followers were jailed for years but no charges could be laid and they were freed.

▶ In 1858 some tribes in the north united and elected a Maori king, hoping that with a single leader instead of many tribes, they would gain recognition. But under the Treaty they had made the English monarch sovereign of New Zealand.

EMPIRE AND ANZAC

New Zealanders, including some Maori, were proud to be part of the British Empire, which set the patterns for family, dress, home and garden, education, and arts, as well as the form of government and English as the official language. Although the British Parliament offered independence in 1931, it was 1947 before New Zealand accepted. It chose to keep its ties with Britain, and the Queen as head of state and became a member of the Commonwealth of Nations. The Maori, though, now distrusted Britain and looked to their tribal leaders, new religions, and young educated Maori to lead them into a new era.

▲ Richard Pearce invented one of the first "air machines" in the world. He flew it in 1903 (it is thought before the Wright brothers) and fifteen years before New Zealand had cars.

◄ The great sheep stations were split into small family farms and dairy farming became New Zealand's leading business. Refrigerated shipping had made Britain the main market for meat, butter, and cheese.

▼ A bride and groom say goodbye to guests in front of a hotel in one of the many towns growing up in the early 1900s.

ERUERA TIRIKATENE'S PLEA

By 1932 followers of one of the Maori religions, Ratana, had elected four Maori Members of Parliament. One of them, Eruera Tirikatene, placed four items before the prime minister and explained their meaning. He said:

A potato was the ordinary Maori who needed land "because a potato cannot grow without soil."

A broken watch was the old law meant to protect Maori land—this broken law must be repaired by the government.

The *tiki* represented the spirit of the Maori people.

So, if the prime minister protected Maori rights he would win the right to wear the *huia* feather, sign of a chief.

In the first fifty years of the new century, internal disasters and world events affected all New Zealanders: there were deaths from epidemics and earthquakes, and a worldwide depression brought poverty and workers' strikes. New Zealand and Australian troops (ANZACs) fought in two world wars, losing many lives but bringing glory to themselves and their nations. When world prices rose, New Zealand was first to offer welfare assistance in low-rental state housing and free health care.

▲ ANZAC Cove, Turkey bears the name of the Australian and New Zealand Army Corps (ANZAC) whose courage at this place made them famous.

ANZAC

On 25 April 1915 the ANZACs landed at Gallipoli. Their great courage and skill is honored each year on ANZAC Day, a national day of remembrance which includes all those who fought in World War I, World War II, Malaya, Korea, Vietnam, and other wars.

◄ In 1923, as part of a state health care program, free milk and dental care were supplied for all school children.

▲ Service medals, World War II.

▼ The World Depression of the 1930s hit New Zealand badly. By 1933 food and housing was poor and scarce and 81,000 men were out of work. Some earned small wages fencing, digging drains, and making roads on government "relief" projects.

► General Freyburg led the New Zealand Division in World War II (1939–1945). Highly decorated, he became the first New Zealand-born Governor General.

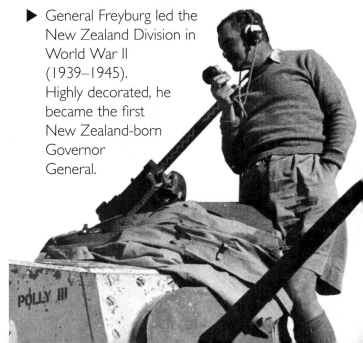

A NATION STANDS

The post-war years were prosperous. New Zealanders had a new sense of their own nationhood and one of the highest standards of living in the world. Ninety percent of farm produce was sold to Britain. This secure market was lost when Britain joined the European Economic Community (EEC) in 1973 and combined with high oil prices caused New Zealand to have ten years of recession, unemployment, social problems, and changes of government. New markets were developed in Asia, Australia, and the Pacific, and these, with growth in tourism, lifted New Zealand's economy by the 1990s. Maori population began to rise, and their demands for change led to new consideration of land claims and cultural recognition.

▲ Sir Edmund Hillary in 1953, with his Sherpa guide Tensing Norgay, was the first to reach the summit of Mount Everest, the world's highest mountain. Other international expeditions included the first crossing of the Antarctic continent.

▶ In 1975, Dame Whina Cooper and her grand-daughter, Irenee, joined some 5,000 others in a Maori land march from the far north to Wellington 688 miles (1,100 kilometers). Parliament set up the Waitangi Land Claims Tribuna, and in 1990, offered to pay one billion dollars, but the Maori did not accept it.

▶ In 1967 decimal coinage replaced pounds, shillings, and pence with dollars and cents. The new dollar was equivalent to ten of the old shillings.

▶ Maori cultural museums were opened. This is a meeting house.

▶ From the 1950s on, technology drove new industries. Refrigerators replaced ice boxes, and washing machines and television sets were soon widely available.

Hello!
Kia ora!

Jet air travel and television brought much greater contact with the rest of the world. Confronted by new issues, New Zealanders stood alone against nuclear testing in the Pacific, and protested against environmental issues and the sending of troops to the Vietnam War. Increased immigration from Asia and the intake of refugees caused a sharp rise in population.

"SOMEONE HAS TO PROTEST! HAVE YOU EVER THOUGHT WHAT UNDERGROUND TESTS COULD DO TO ME?"

▲ New Zealanders protested when France began to test nuclear explosions on the Pacific island of Muroroa. Major protests are set out below:

● 1972: small boats sailed into the test.

● 1973: the government ordered naval ships into the danger area and won worldwide attention.

● 1984: established a nuclear-free zone of 200 miles (320 kilometers) around the country's shores.

● 1985: The Greenpeace ship *Rainbow Warrior* was sunk in Auckland's harbor by French Secret Service. Worldwide protests forced France to sign a comprehensive Test Ban Treaty.

● 1987: nuclear-armed or nuclear-powered warships were prohibited in New Zealand waters.

LANGUAGES

In 1987 the *Maori Language Act* made Maori an official language of New Zealand. Maori now appears beside English on many documents. For example:

> National Library of New Zealand
> *Te Puna Matauranga o Aotearoa*

MAORI is from the Malayo-Polynesian (or Austronesian) family of languages spoken on thousands of islands in Oceania.

There are some differences in dialect, but different groups can talk to each other. For example, when James Cook arrived, Tupia, a Polynesian man who had joined the ship, could still speak with the Maori in New Zealand even though they had been isolated from Polynesia for about 400 years.

The Maori language in its written form uses the English alphabet.

ENGLISH as New Zealand's official language has brought many advantages. It is the official language of about forty-five other nations, and the most widely used language of trade and commerce (on which New Zealand's economy depends). And it opens a rich world of books and information. Originating from the Indo-European family of languages, English is a living language and continues to change, enriched by many other languages. In New Zealand, it absorbs Maori words and place names and also words introduced by technology and modern migrants from Europe and Asia.

GOVERNMENT

New Zealand is governed by a system of parliamentary democracy based on the British Westminster system (which took its principles from laws from the Bible's Old Testament). It recognizes the value of the individual human being and his or her right to voice an opinion. Because everyone cannot attend Parliament, the people elect representatives who speak and vote on their behalf. The members of Parliament can act as individuals or as members of a party. The party with the majority of elected members forms the Government. Other members, known as the Opposition have a duty to watch that laws are properly carried out and the rights of the people upheld.

HOUSE FOR A DEMOCRATIC PARLIAMENT

▼ Parliament House is a building where the Government and Opposition work. One of their most important roles is to make laws or change or abolish existing laws. A proposed law is set out in a bill which is "read" before the parliament three times before it becomes law. Between readings the bill is studied in detail, amended and debated. Only then can it be voted into law.

▶ Members vote on important issues such as a bill, by passing through either the "ayes" or the "no's" door.

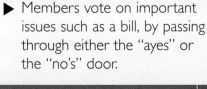

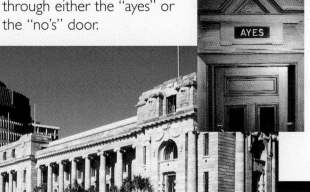

▲ ▶ Central workroom of the democratic parliament is the debating chamber of the House of Representatives (seen here from the Speaker's Chair). The Government is seated on the Speaker's right and the Opposition on the left. The room is arranged for debate from two or more different points of view. The Speaker controls the debate.

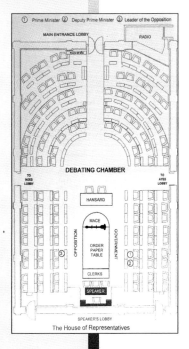

① Prime Minister ② Deputy Prime Minister ③ Leader of the Opposition

MAIN ENTRANCE LOBBY RADIO

DEBATING CHAMBER

TO NO'S LOBBY — TO AYES LOBBY

HANSARD

MACE

ORDER PAPER TABLE

OPPOSITION — GOVERNMENT

CLERKS

SPEAKER

SPEAKER'S LOBBY

The House of Representatives

◀ THE FLAG

The four-stars of the Southern Cross are visible only in the southern hemisphere. They have been a guiding constellation above the vast oceans crossed by peoples of both Maori and European descent. The British Union flag recognizes British culture in such areas as law and government, literature, and science.

▶ Freedom of speech allows individuals or newpapers to comment on personalities and issues. When this cartoon was drawn, the government had barred nuclear-armed or nuclear-powered warships from New Zealand waters. This strong stand cost New Zealand its place on ANZUS, an alliance between Australia, New Zealand, and the United States. (See also page 25).

A WELFARE GOVERNMENT SYSTEM

New Zealand has a welfare system, which means that the government owns most services. It also collects taxes and then provides the funds and programs it deems best for the people.

To meet its welfare promises the government must ensure that the country has a strong economy with good overseas sales. The people must be able to earn enough to pay the taxes.

▼ This albatross chick on Campbell Island benefits from funded Conservation Department expertise on island wildlife and environment.

▼ Most of the nation's 2,300 primary schools and 330 secondary schools are supported by the state. Private schools are funded by students' fees.

▼ Public facilities, like libraries and hospitals, and also individuals, such as the elderly and unemployed, all depend on the government for funds.

NEW ZEALAND AND THE WORLD

The isolation and small size of New Zealand's population has not prevented its people from achieving daring and noteworthy success in the wider world. Great curiosity about the unknown and courage to strike out toward it were always traits of both Maori and European settlers. British education and ties with Britain first gave New Zealanders opportunity to extend their ability and practical skills within the established European culture. But now New Zealanders have wider contacts with many other countries and continue their long term comradeship and friendly rivalry with Australians.

▲ Queen Elizabeth II opening the New Zealand Parliament in Wellington. She is wearing a kiwi-feather chieftain's cloak denoting her status as Queen (the head of state) of New Zealand.

▶ Dame Kiri Te Kanawa (1944–) opera and concert singer is one of the world's most acclaimed and popular lyric sopranos. She has appeared with London's Royal Opera, New York's Metropolitan Opera, the Munich Opera, and other major opera houses worldwide and has made many recordings.

◀ Out of a national love of boats came the skilled sailors and boat-builders who won the America's Cup in 1995 in American waters, and retained it in 1999–2000 at home in Hauraki Gulf.

▼ King penguins in simulated Antarctic conditions. The International Antarctic Centre at Christchurch is a supply and administration base for American, Italian, and New Zealand research programs.

▲ New Zealand's thoroughbred horses were well known overseas as a Light Horse Brigade during World War I, then as champions in horse sports—here competing in the cross-country event of the Sydney 2000 Olympics.

▲ These Samoan singers wait their turn to perform. Some 150,000 immigrants from Pacific Islands live in Auckland. Up to 11,000 Western Samoan citizens may be granted residence each year.

As a member of the Commonwealth of Nations New Zealand is one of some fifty member nations that consult and cooperate for the "common weal" (an old English term meaning "for the good of all"). Polynesians are increasingly looking to New Zealand as their major center for work and education.

ENVIRONMENTAL ACTION

In the Wellington Maritime Museum you can play a computer oil-spill game. The aim is to save the coastline.

You can see some of New Zealand's concerns about the environment by reading this long list of international agreements that it has signed:

Antarctic-Environmental Protocol, Antarctic-Marine Living Resources, Antarctic Treaty, Biodiversity, Climate Change, Desertification, Endangered Species, Environmental Modification, Hazardous Wastes, Law of the Sea, Marine Dumping, Nuclear Test Ban, Ozone Layer Protection, Ship Pollution, Tropical Timber, Wetlands, Whaling.

▲ Rugby Union football is New Zealand's national sport. Its famous team, the All Blacks, are leaders in international Rugby. Here, they play Australia for the Bledisloe Cup, an ongoing and hard-fought contest between the two countries.

▶ Tuatara, the only surviving species of an otherwise extinct reptile family, is protected under a recovery program.

FARMERS OF LAND AND SEA

Research and technology have helped New Zealand to establish a world-wide reputation as a producer of high quality agricultural products. Farmers combine effective management of soil, pasture, and stock with the temperate climate and fertile lands. Machinery and equipment are costly since they must be imported. Primary producers suffered the loss of their greatest market when England joined the European Economic Community (EEC). However, the farmers have been quick to innovate and develop new crops such as fruit, vegetables, and flowers, which are suitable for new markets nearer home.

▲ Prime wool and fat lambs are the traditional leaders of New Zealand's primary products. Much grazing land is being converted from dairy and sheep farming to horticulture.

► Research and testing help to produce better crops and livestock.

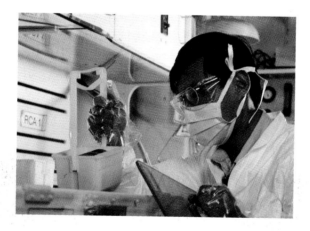

▼ Cultivated farms on the Canterbury Plains, which were formed by silt and gravel carried by three large rivers from the Southern Alps.

▼ Ducks, geese, and other birdlife are attracted to the pasturelands.

▲ Deer, introduced in the 1800s, caused damage to the hills of the South Island by stripping natural growth and eroding soil. Since the 1970s, deer farmers have marketed venison and antler velvet, mainly in countries of the Far East.

MAIN PRIMARY PRODUCTS

AGRICULTURAL PRODUCTS: wheat, barley, potatoes, pulses, fruits, vegetables, wool, beef, dairy products, fish.

EXPORT COMMODITIES: dairy products, meat, fish, wool, forestry products, manufactured products.

EXPORT PARTNERS: Australia 22%, United States 14%, Japan 13%, United Kingdom (Britain) 7% (1999 figures).

▲ Fruits such as citrus,
▼ raspberries, kiwifruit, olives, strawberries, and tamarillos grow in the north.

◀ Cheese is one of the excellent dairy foods exported.

▲ Pastures and forest reach to the water's edge in the rich volcanic soil of the north.

▶ Eight million cattle produce high quality beef, a leading export food.

◀ Fishing has provided healthy food from earliest settlement. It is also a long-time favorite sport. Ocean fish such as swordfish, marlin, shark, and yellowtail abound in the waters off the northeast coast.

▶ Lucerne is delivered to a geothermal drying plant that makes high-protein stock feed.

INDUSTRY AND COMMERCE

Since Britain, once New Zealand's major market, turned to the EEC (see page 24) for fresh foods, New Zealand has increased its industry and trade with Australia, Japan, and America. Natural resources being developed include iron ore, sand, coal, timber, hydropower, natural gas, gold, and limestone. Key industries include forestry, fisheries, tanneries, cement works and fertilizer factories, a steel works, aluminium smelter, and oil refinery. Technology and tourism are now leading industries.

▲ Modern technology is utilized in commerce. For example, this land survey business is engaged in major projects, such as airport landing strips in New Zealand and overseas.

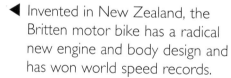

▶ The fashion industry is achieving recognition for its innovative design, especially in fine wool garments and specialist camping, trekking, and ski gear.

▲ Marketing natural or manufactured products to overseas markets is an essential part of commerce.

◀ Invented in New Zealand, the Britten motor bike has a radical new engine and body design and has won world speed records.

▼ Radiata pine trees are grown for timber (9,100 per day can be cut).

▼ Trucks deliver the pine logs for milling; the logs go on to timber yards for local use or wharves for export markets.

▼ Stockpiles of sawdust awaiting shipment to the pulp and paper mill at Kawerau near Rotorua.

▼ Machined wood and greenstone supply the souvenir market, but hand-work is valued.

▲ New Zealand glass and pottery have reached high artistic and technical standards and have a place in worldwide collections.

TOURISM INDUSTRY

New Zealand is an ideal vacation spot and many people are employed in making travel easy and enjoyable. Roads, transport, food, and accommodation are some of the travel industries. People who take part in outdoor and adventure sports often invent, manufacture, or sell equipment.

▲ Technology and engineering are combined with knowledge of skiing and the snowfields to make and install a ski lift.

◄ Manufacture of safety wear and inflatable white-water rafts are industries linked to tourism.

PERCENT OF PEOPLE IN LABOR OCCUPATIONS
Of a total of 1.88 million people working in the year 2000, 10% worked in agriculture, 25% in industry, and 65% in services (1995 estimate).

▶ When gold is purified by smelting at high temperatures, it becomes liquid and fills ingot molds. The residue is caught in a sand tray.

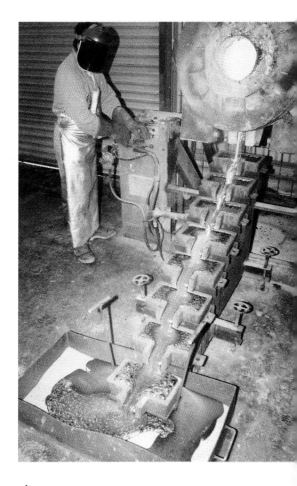

▲ Geothermal steam tapped from the volcanic plateau of the North Island is one source of electrical power. Hydro power plants are the major producers of power.

▼ Open cut gold-mining in Martha Mine produces gold and silver worth about one million dollars (NZ) each week.

WELLINGTON AND AUCKLAND

Wellington was chosen as the national capital in 1865 because it was central to both islands. Parliamentary buildings, business and shopping are centered on flat reclaimed land overlooking a large harbor (see page 19), and beyond, high-rise and older houses climb surrounding hillsides. From the tops of these hills one can see the South Island and the city below, with its art gallery, botanical gardens, museums, zoo, waterfront marinas, and container terminal.

▲ Museum of New Zealand, *Te papa Tongarewa*, one of the largest new museums in the world, houses exhibits of the nation's history, culture and environment.

▶ Plimmer, the man called "father of Wellington."

◀ City high-rise buildings are engineered to resist earthquakes.

▶ Kate Sheppard (1848–1934) fought against excessive alcohol-drinking, which caused abuse of women, and her leadership made New Zealand, in 1893, the first country to give women the vote.

▶ Parliament buildings and National Library complex.

▶ Outdoor concerts are popular.

▼ Ferries cross Cook Strait between the North and South islands. Fierce air flows in the strait make a "windy Wellington."

The city of Auckland spreads across a narrow volcanic isthmus between two large natural harbors, which on weekends are alive with waterside shoppers and every kind of boat heading for the islands and beaches of the Hauraki Gulf. Auckland was the national capital before 1865. Now it is the largest city and major point of entry for visitors. It handles the bulk of the nation's import and export business. There is fast growth of population with many migrants, especially from Asia and Polynesia.

▲
Old Town Hall clock tower is a landmark.

▲ Life in the city: cultural dance on the museum steps. . .

▶ . . . escaping the office for lunch in the sun. . .

◀ ▼ ▶
. . . collector's markets, cafes, music, restaurants.

▲ Auckland city center rises between Waitemata and Manukau harbors.

▼ . . . street trees, parks and gardens, and shopping malls. . .

BEING "KIWI"

Aware of the latest international trends but proud of their own country, New Zealanders (who cheerfully call themselves "Kiwis") are both travelers and home lovers. They are casual in many ways, hospitable, and proud of their culture, but not afraid to reject or debate issues that concern them either in their own country or in the world. Used to managing on their own, Kiwis use their initiative in small ways, like inventing a gate latch, or in the larger world arena in music, science, or sports technology.

▶ The kiwi is the national symbol, said to have been first used as a nickname for New Zealanders in 1905, when the All Blacks rugby football team defeated Britain.

▲ Fishing is a national skill.

▼ Being Kiwi is to link your craft closely to the land; creating pottery from clay, woven fabrics from wool, glass from sands, and carvings from bone, wood, and stone

▲ New Zealanders make use of computers and the internet to overcome distance in global business and communications.

▼ Sailing at all ages is very Kiwi.

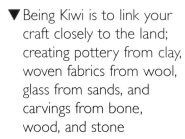

◀ . . . or refining classic Maori woodcarving at the Maori Arts and Crafts Institute.

New Zealanders place a high value on taking part in activities that challenge and inspire them, whether it is in hard physical effort on the sports field, viewing works of art in a city gallery, or building and repairing their homes. Differences between the various cultures are maturing into an appreciation of what each has to offer.

▲ Parachuting, parapenting and bungee jumping thrill many Kiwis who, although flightless, love to fly!

▶
A close-knit community recalling its history by the reenactment of important events.

▲ Playing around a giant obelisk on One-Tree Hill, Auckland, which is part of open parklands given to the city in honor of the Maori people.

▼ Flower gardening is a favorite pastime that came, like the rose, from Britain.

◀ Being Kiwi is building a "bach" (tiny holiday hut) near a lake, river, beach, or bushland as a base for family day trips and holidays

▼ . . . but most of all, it is a home of your own in a peaceful place where you are free.

▲ Promises of commitment are made in a marriage ceremony, usually in a church, with friends and family as witnesses. Afterward there is a lavish meal where speeches are made and gifts given to the newly married couple.

FAMILY LIVING

Family is central to the culture of New Zealand. The *whanau* (family unit) is the most important part of Maori society and to a large extent is still linked to the *iwi* (see page 14). Important concerns are often discussed within the extended family group. In general, parents and children live in their own house. European background families decide their own affairs, but keep in contact with extended family. Many care for grandparents or share a house with them. In many homes both parents work and in others, one parent cares for the children. Families who have come from other countries often have to learn a new language and different lifestyle. They also introduce new ideas that become part of the culture, especially when people from different backgrounds marry. This normally safe and beautiful land is a wonderful place for families.

▲ Families meet over a meal on special occasions, like birthdays, or perhaps to comfort each other in times of need.

▶ Grandparents have a role in developing family values and a sense of belonging. They also often act as after-school caregivers for the children of working parents.

◀ Learning about each other.

▲ Family and friends meet in a dance group

▼ . . . and teens know what small people like to do.

◀ ▲ "I remember how we slid down the snow in our yellow raincoats."

▲ Although 80% of New Zealanders live in cities, many people grew up on farms, and children visit them on vactions or school trips.

◀ Pipi shells.

ENVIRONMENT AND MEMORIES

New Zealanders have the good fortune to live in a healthy and self-contained land. Although they have won honor and felt grief in two world wars and some internal wars and troubles, the country has not suffered like those with a history of fierce invasions. The land has endless delightful places to live or vacation, and most children have happy childhood memories of close contact with nature. In general, these experiences produce a relaxed people.

▶ "In the summer holidays we camped by the water."

◀ "We found tiny shellfish in rockpools and pipis in the sand."

FRESH AND ABUNDANT FOOD

Food is plentiful and of high quality. Dairy foods such as milk, cheese, butter, and yogurt, fresh every day, are served with cereals, fruit, and vegetables. There are pasture-fed Canterbury lamb, beef, and venison, deep sea kingfish and marlin from the Bay of Islands, mussels from Marlborough Sound, Lake Taupo trout or crayfish, and blue cod from Fiordland. Maori traditional foods include freshwater eels, pipi, tuatua, and steamed vegetables. Pies, porridge, roast meats and vegetables, breads, and "fish-n-chips" are typical dishes from Britain. Many people now want organic and vegetarian foods and new tastes have come with immigrants and tourists from Asia and Europe. Home-cooked family meals are normal, but cafes, restaurants, and fast food are very popular.

▲
Each kiwifruit contains a day's supply of vitamin C.

▼
Knife, fork, and paper napkin for an outdoor buffet (a serve-yourself) meal.

◄ ▲
Traditional English favorites —a cup of tea and apple pie served with ice cream or thickly whipped cream.

▶ Home cooking is central to family and friends' get-togethers such as lunch on Sunday, a birthday with cake-cutting, Christmas dinner with all the trimmings, or a casual outdoor meal.

▼ Mint, grown in a pot near the back door, is picked to make mint sauce for roast lamb. Other herbs used in traditional dishes include chives, rosemary, marjoram, and thyme.

◄ A giant fish with lobsters is a chef's delight as a centerpiece for a special occasion.

▲ Tangelos, a sweet citrus, and many other fruits fill market stalls.

▲

There is always a spot to enjoy an extended family meal. On warm days, it's a picnic or barbecue at a park, beach, or bush area. On cold, wet days, "take-aways" are popular.

▲ Green vegetables are often picked from home gardens.

◀ Breads and many foods from Europe and the Mediterranean, as well as from Asia, are enjoyed.

COOKING A *HANGI*

A Maori *hangi*, or earth oven, is ideal for catering for a large group of people. Everyone helps prepare. While the women wrap morsels of meat, seafood, and vegetables in leaves, the men dig a pit and heat large, smooth stones in a log fire. The stones are placed in the bottom of the pit, with wet sacking over them, and then baskets of leaf-wrapped food are placed on top and covered with soil. After about two hours the steamed food is tender and the feast begins.

▼ On the snowfields hot dishes eaten in the sun are perfect.

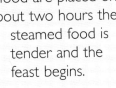

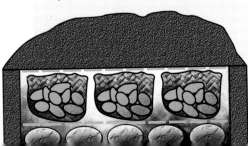

EDUCATION

New Zealanders place a high value on education, from early childhood learning programs to adult education courses, but they are also aware that all education does not occur in formal classes. For example, early education includes programs such as Playgroup, Maori *Te Kohunga Reo* (Language Nest), and Pacific Island languages. In both government-funded and private fee-paying schools, essential learning areas include language, mathematics, science, and technology, social sciences, arts, health, and physical wellbeing. Children must attend school until they are 16 years old. Many continue to 18 years to gain university entrance. New Zealand has one of the world's highest literacy rates, with 99 percent English literacy.

▲ After preschool, primary includes juniors (ages 5 and 6), middle school (7 and 8), intermediate (11 and 12), followed by secondary school from 13 years on up.

◄ Love of books and reading begins when parents read to their child and give toddlers colorful books to enjoy.

► Groups of children working together on projects in classroom learning centres develop independence and research skills. Primary students can run meetings and co-operate on a project.

◄ Reading areas allow for comfort and relaxed enjoyment. The *Ready to Read* series, used in all New Zealand classrooms, is sold throughout North America, Australia and the Pacific, and the success of *Learning Media* has also gained international recognition.

a   b   c   d   e   f   g   h   i   j   k   l   m   n

▶ The ornate clock tower of Auckland University dates back to 1926. This is one of seven universities that follow the British academic tradition on which New Zealand's education was based.

▲ Arts and crafts, physical and para-medical, or business-oriented courses are offered in technical and degree institutions.

▼ In secondary school there is a choice of subjects and levels of study.

◀ On graduation day university students who have completed their courses of study (usually at least four years) wear cap and gown and are presented with a certificate stating their professional qualifications.

WIDER LEARNING EXPERIENCES

Discovery through exploration, observation, and discussion is a key factor in the learning process. Field trips, school excursions, and access to museums provide hands-on experiences.

◀ Researching and reporting information gathered at a museum.

▲ Computer skills are taught at most schools and in tertiary business and technology courses.

▼ Solving puzzles and finding "how it works."

o p q r s t u v w x y z

▲ A tree fern canopy. *Ponga*, or silver fern is New Zealand's plant emblem.

VISITING NEW ZEALAND

Within the islands of New Zealand it is safe and friendly and easy to travel. Never far from mountains or sea, you can climb a volcano, walk beside steaming pools, or fish and swim along streams and beaches. Crossing between islands, sleep on a ferry and drive to glaciers and snow fields, or, further south, see seals and penguins and the astonishing fjordlands. Join a group for tramping, sailing, and adventure sports. Visit museums, Maori-culture villages, farms, and goldfields as well—all in one country!

▲ There is no better place to load your sleeping bag and go camping. There are roadside barbecues, parks, family units, and huts. Visitors who leave everything litter free are very welcome.

▲ See the skeletons and eggs of extinct giant moas.

◄ At Rotorua thermal activity
▼ sends a geyser spurting high in the air, heats the water in rock pools and the earth in bubbling mud pools, and fills the air with the smell of sulphur.

▼ Eat where you can hear the sound of water falling.

▲ *Poi*, made of flax. Maori women twirl and beat them in time with their stirring song and dance.

▲ Try your hand at gold panning in an old Arrowtown mine.

◀ Maori welcome to a re-created *kainga* and *pa*. The *putatra*, or conch shell, sounds a warning that strangers are approaching. *Poi* are tucked into the waist when not in use.

▲ Mitre Peak plunges far below the deep icy water of Milford Sound.

◀ Underground in the Glow Worm Caves millions of tiny insects shine like far-off stars in the silent total darkness.

▶ Fly to New Zealand's high snowfields and ski cross-country to see such wonders as this ice-cave.

INDEX

How to use the Index
Words in standard type are specific.
Words in **bold** type are general subject references;
the word itself may not appear on each page listed.

Additional information can be found in other titles in the
Ask About Asia series: China, India, Indonesia, Japan, Korea,
Malaysia, Thailand, Vietnam and Ask About Oceania:
Australia, New Zealand.

PICTURE CREDITS

Abbreviations: r = right, l = left,
t = top, c = center, b = below

Noeline Lapwood
Principal photographer. All
images except those listed below:
Peter Barker Maps **9;** **11** bc; **12** bl;
13 tr; **15** cl; **18** cr; **41** bl.
Mike Langford **10** tl, cr; **27** br; **30**
c, bl; **31** c; **35** bcl; **39** c; **41**c.
Maori Arts and Crafts Institute
13 cl; **14** cr; **15** crt; **45** tl.

Tamaki Maori Village Cover;
Title; **8** br; **14** cl; **36** bl; **44** bc.
15 cl (*Moko* T. Mitai-Ngati).
Dein Miskell 10 cl, bc; **22** crt, crb,
brt, brb; **24** br; **39** clb; **37** tc; **40**
clb, crt; **41** bc.
**Christchurch and Canterbury
Marketing 18** cl; **21** tl; **30** cr; **33**
cr; **37** tr; **41** br.
Northland Images Contents; **8** tl,
cr; **13** t; **28** br; **31** br; **37** bc, br; **39**
tl, br; **40** bc; **44** br.

**New Zealand Parliamentary
Service Commission 11** cl; **26** tr,
c, cr, bl; **28** tl; **31** br; **34** br.
Tourism Rotorua 10 cr; **11** tl; **31**
c, crt, crb; **39** tr; **45** cl.
Tourism Holdings 28 br; **33** tr;
45 tr, cr, br.
Tourism Auckland 35 tl, cr.
Totally Wellington 34 cr, bl.
**Dalmation Genealogical Society
20** br; **43** c.
AP/AAP 29 bl.

Mark Samson 33 br.
Decca Records 28 cr.
New Zealand Herald 24 c.
Vineyard Stock 17 br; **29** tl; **32** c;
35 c; **37** bl; **38** bc; **39** tc; **40** clt, bl;
41 cr.

Every effort has been made to
consult all relevant people and
organizations. Any omissions or
errors are unintentional and
should be reported to Vineyard
Freepress Pty Ltd.

Alexander Turnbull Library, Wellington

12 John Webber 1750-93 *Boats of the
Friendly Isles.* Official artist on Cook's third
voyage to the Pacific; **13** Miss King
Phornium tenax, or New Zealand flax;
1842; Frederick William Frohawk
1860–1942 *Dinornis ingens (restoration
from skeleton and feathers 1901);* **14** Sydney
Parkinson 1745–71 *A war canoe of New
Zealand* London 1784; **16** Isaac Gilsemans
A view of Murderers Bay 1642; Francis J.B.
Bayldon *Dimensional sketch of HMS
Endeavour, Captain James Cook.* 1923;
Nathaniel Dance Holland, 1734–1811

Captain Cook.; Louis John Steele
1843–1918 *Arrival of Captain Cook, an
incident at the Bay of Islands.* 1890; **17**
Sydney Parkinson 1745–71 *Botanical plates
relating to Cook's first voyage (Kowhai);*
Rigobert Bonne 1727–95 *Carte de Nouvelle
Zeelande.* 1778; **18** James Barry *The Rev
Thomas Kendall and the Maori chiefs Hongi
and Waikato.* 1820; Philip Walsh
1843–1914 *Sketch of Bishop and Mrs Cowie
travelling in North Auckland;* Alfred John
Cooper d. 1869 *Maori kainga with cleared
fields at Te Arakanihi 1855;* **19** Leonard
Cornwall Mitchell 1901–71 *A*

*reconstruction of the signing of the Treaty of
Waitangi.* 1840; William Potts 1859–1947
City of Wellington NZ 1885; **20** Alfred John
Cooper d.1869 *Bushwork. Cross-cutting
timber* c. 1860; **21** *Group outside a timber
camp;* Arthur David McCormick
1860–1943 *Heke fells the flagstaff at
Kororareka.* 1908; G. M. Preston Collection
*Tukaroto Matutaera Potatau Te
Wherowhero Tawhiao, second Maori king;*
Philip Walsh 1843–1914 *Arrest of Maori
ploughmen on Jury's farm at Tikorangi in
1879;* **23** Horace Millichamp Moore-Jones
1878–1922 *Anzac Cove; the historic landing*

*place from a sketch made by Sapper H.
Moore-Jones 1915; Auckland school children
drinking milk; Men building a fence during
the Depression; General Freyburg on tank
turret, Second World War;* **24** John Cecil
Hill *Sir Edmund Hillary* 1919– ; Gordon
Burt *Refrigerator advertisement;* **25** Eric
Walmsley Heath 1923– 'Someone has to
protest ...'; **27** Nevile Sidney Lodge 1918–89
'I just never thought ...' 12 December 1986;
Phillip George Poppleton *Sooty albatross,
Campbell Island. 1950;* **36** Trevor Lloyd
1863–1937 *Britain defeated by the All
Blacks.* 1905.